Die deutsche Grammatik klar gemacht

Karl F. Otto, Jr.
University of Pennsylvania

Keri L. Bryant
Murray State University

Wolff von Schmidt
University of Utah

Editor in Chief: Steve Debow
Executive Editor: Laura McKenna
Director of Development: Marian Wassner
Assistant Editor: María F. García
Editorial Assistant: Karen George

Managing Editor: Debbie Brennan
Graphic Project Manager: Ximena de la Piedra
Manufacturing Buyer: Tricia Kenny

© 1996 by Prentice Hall, Inc.
A Simon and Schuster Company
Upper Saddle River, New Jersey 07458

Printed in the United States of America
10 9 8 7 6 5 4 3 2

ISBN   0-13-328154-X

Prentice Hall International (UK) Limited, *London*
Prentice Hall of Australia Pty. Limited, *Sydney*
Prentice Hall Canada Inc., *Toronto*
Prentice Hall Hispanoamericana, S. A., *México*
Prentice Hall of India Private Limited, *New Delhi*
Prentice Hall of Japan, Inc., *Tokyo*
Simon & Schuster Asia Pte. Ltd., *Singapore*
Editora Prentice Hall do Brasil, Ltda., *Rio de Janeiro*

Table of Contents

1. Nouns and articles

1.1 Gender and case

All German nouns have one of three genders:

1. Masculine (**der**)
2. Feminine (**die**)
3. Neuter (**das**)

Since the gender of German nouns is generally unpredictable, it is best to memorize the proper gender with each noun you learn.

German has four cases. These cases and their primary uses are:

1. **NOMINATIVE CASE**	SUBJECT OF SENTENCE:	**Das Kleid** ist teuer.
	SUBJECT OF CLAUSE:	Ich weiß, daß **das Kleid** teuer ist.
	PREDICATE NOMINATIVE:	Der Mann ist **mein Vater**.
2. **ACCUSATIVE CASE**	DIRECT OBJECT (RECIPIENT OF THE ACTION OF THE VERB):	Kennst du **diese Frau**?
	OBJECT OF PREPOSITION:	Ich arbeite für **meine Tante**.
3. **DATIVE CASE**	INDIRECT OBJECT (THE PERSON OR THING TO WHOM OR FOR WHOM SOMETHING IS DONE):	Gib **deiner Schwester** das Buch!
	OBJECT OF PREPOSITION:	Ich spreche mit **meinem Sohn**.
4. **GENITIVE CASE**	POSSESSION:	Die Wohnung **meiner Freundin** ist sehr klein.

1.2 Articles

Each gender has distinctive forms for both the definite articles (*the*) and the indefinite articles (*a, an*).

Definite articles (the *der*-words)

	MASC.	FEM.	NEUT.	PL.
NOM.	der	die	das	die
ACC.	den	die	das	die
DAT.	dem	der	dem	den
GEN.	des	der	des	der

Several other words, commonly referred to as **der**-words, have the same declension as the definite article.

alle	*all*
beide	*both*
dieser	*this, that (the latter)*; (pl.) *these*
jeder	*each, every*
jener	*that (the former)*; (pl.) *those*
mancher	(sg., uncommon) *many a*; (pl.) *some, several*
solcher	(sg., uncommon) *such a*; (pl.) *such*
welcher	*which*

Bei **diesem Wetter** bleiben wir zu Hause.
Die Lehrerin hat **beiden Kindern** geholfen.

Indefinite articles (the *ein*-words)

	MASC.	FEM.	NEUT.	PL.
NOM.	ein	eine	ein	keine
ACC.	einen	eine	ein	keine
DAT.	einem	einer	einem	keinen
GEN.	eines	einer	eines	keiner

Several other words, commonly referred to as **ein**-words, have the same declension as the indefinite article.

mein	*my*
dein	*your* (familiar singular)
sein	*his, its*
ihr	*her, its*
unser	*our*
euer	*your* (familiar plural)
ihr	*their*
Ihr	*your* (formal, singular and plural)
kein	*no, not a, not any*

Heute habe ich **keine** Zeit.
Sind Sie mit **Ihrem** Auto zufrieden?

1.3 Noun plurals

German nouns have several patterns of plural formations; it is therefore best to memorize the plural of each noun as you learn the noun itself. The five most common plural patterns are:

no change or ¨:	das Zimmer, **die Zimmer**; die Mutter, **die Mütter**
-e or ¨e:	der Besuch, **die Besuche**; die Kuh, **die Kühe**
-er or ¨er:	das Kind, **die Kinder**; das Buch, **die Bücher**
-en, -n, or -nen:	die Zeitung, **die Zeitungen**; die Katze, **die Katzen**
	die Studentin, **die Studentinnen**
-s:	das Auto, **die Autos**

1.4 Noun declensions and weak nouns

Apart from the plural indicators, there are only two endings applied to nouns. They are:

Genitive singular masculine and neuter: adds -s or -es to the nominative form: **das Haus meines Vaters.**[1]

Dative plural (all genders): adds -n or -en to the nominative plural form: **mit den Kindern, unter den Betten.**[2] Exception: nouns whose plurals already end in -n or end in -s: **mit den Katzen, hinter den Autos.**

One group of German nouns has an -en ending in all cases but the nominative singular. These nouns are masculine in gender; they often denote living beings and end in -e (**der Junge, der Kollege**), or they are nouns of non-German origin, ending in -and, -arch, -ent, -et, -graph, -ist, -log, or -soph (**der Journalist, der Philosoph**). These nouns are often called weak nouns or masculine -n nouns. They are declined as follows:

	SINGULAR	PLURAL
NOM.	der Student	die Studenten
ACC.	den Studenten	die Studenten
DAT.	dem Studenten	den Studenten
GEN.	des Studenten	der Studenten

---

[1]The **-es** ending is usually added when the noun is monosyllabic (**das Haus des Mannes**); it is required when the noun ends in **s, ß, sch,** or **z** (**die Farbe des Schulhauses**).

[2]In the dative, an **-e** is added to masculine and neuter nouns in certain fixed expressions: **auf dem Lande, nach Hause.**

2. Pronouns

Pronouns are words that replace or refer to nouns.

2.1 Personal pronouns

Personal pronouns refer to both people and things. They agree in gender and number with the nouns to which they refer.

NOMINATIVE	ACCUSATIVE	DATIVE	GENITIVE [3]
ich (*I*)	mich	mir	meiner
du (*you*, fam. sg.)	dich	dir	deiner
er (*he, it*)	ihn	ihm	seiner
sie (*she, it*)	sie	ihr	ihrer
es (*it, he, she*)	es	ihm	seiner
wir (*we*)	uns	uns	unser
ihr (*you*, fam. pl.)	euch	euch	euer
sie (*they*)	sie	ihnen	ihrer
Sie (*you*, formal sg. + pl.)	Sie	Ihnen	Ihrer

Sie hat ihn geschlagen.	*She hit him.*
Geben Sie mir die Butter, bitte.	*Please give me the butter.*

Remember that German has three forms of you: **du** (singular) and **ihr** (plural) for those with whom one is on a first-name basis, **Sie** for more formal relationships.

Note, too, that English *it* may be equivalent to any of the three genders in German: **er, sie, es**. Which of these is needed will be determined by the gender of the noun referred to:

Der Tisch ist sauber.	**Er** ist sauber.
Die Sonne scheint heute.	**Sie** scheint heute.
Das Wetter ist schön.	**Es** ist schön.

The common idiomatic phrase **es gibt** means *there is* or *there are*. It is always followed by the accusative case.

Es gibt viele Ausländer in Deutschland.
There are many foreigners in Germany.

In diesem Zimmer **gibt es** nur einen Stuhl.
There is only one chair in this room.

---

[3]These forms are provided only for the sake of completeness; they are rarely used in contemporary German.

Die deutsche Grammatik klar gemacht

2.2 Possessive pronouns

The possessive pronouns (also called possessive adjectives) are all declined like the so-called **ein**-words; they are:

mein	*my*	**unser**	*our*
dein	*your*, fam. sg.	**euer**	*your*
sein	*his, its*	**ihr**	*their*
ihr	*her, its*		
	Ihr	*your*	

Meine Noten sind dieses Jahr sehr schlecht.
Hast du **unsren**[4] **Professor** gesehen?

2.3 Relative pronouns

In both German and English, relative clauses provide additional information about a previously mentioned person, thing, or idea. These relative clauses are joined to the main clause by a relative pronoun that refers to a noun or pronoun in the preceding clause.

MAIN CLAUSE	RELATIVE CLAUSE
Hier ist **der Brief**,	**den** ich von meiner Mutter bekommen habe.
Here's the letter	*(that) I got from my mother.*
Das ist **die Politikerin**,	**mit der** ich zur Schule gegangen bin.
That's the politician	*with whom I went to school.*

English relative pronouns are words such as *who(m)*, *that*, *which*, etc. German relative pronouns consist of forms of the definite article; they have gender, number, and case.[5] Gender and number are determined by the antecedent (the noun to which the relative pronoun refers). Case is determined by the function of the relative pronoun within the clause. Relative pronouns are declined exactly like the **der**-words, except for the dative plural and the genitive.

	MASC.	FEM.	NEUT.	PL.
NOM.	der	die	das	die
ACC.	den	die	das	die
DAT.	dem	der	dem	denen
GEN.	dessen	deren	dessen	deren

---

[4]When **euer** and **unser** add endings, the last **e** in the original word is often dropped: **unsre Heimat**, **euren Wagen** (acc.).

[5]Occasionally **welch-** is used as a relative pronoun as well.

Ist das **der Kuli, den** ich gestern gekauft habe?

Den is used, because it refers to **Kuli** (masculine singular) and it functions as the direct object within the relative clause (accusative).

Kommt **die Studentin, die** neben dir sitzt, aus der Schweiz?

Die is used, because it refers to **Studentin** (feminine singular) and it functions as the subject of the relative clause (nominative).

Sind das **die Frauen, mit denen** du arbeitest?

Denen is used, because it refers to **Frauen** (plural) and it functions as the dative object of a preposition.

In German, all relative clauses are set off by commas. Note that they use dependent word order, with the verb in final position. In addition—unlike English—the relative pronoun can never be omitted from the sentence; and if a preposition is used, it must be the first word in the clause.

If a relative pronoun has no specific antecedent, it can be expressed by **wer/wen/wem/ wessen** (*who, whom, whoever,* etc.) or **was** (*what, whatever, which,* etc.).

Ich weiß nicht, **wer** das gemacht hat.
I don't know who did that.

Sie kommt heute nicht, **was** mich sehr traurig macht.
She is not coming today, which makes me very sad.

The neuter relative pronoun **was** must also be used whenever the antecedent is an indefinite pronoun (**alles, etwas, manches, nichts, vieles,** etc.) or a neuter superlative used as a noun (**das Beste, das Schönste,** etc.).

Sie erzählte alles, **was** wichtig war.
She explained everything that was important.

Es war das Beste, **was** ich machen konnte.
It was the best (that) I could do.

2.4 Demonstrative pronouns

Demonstrative pronouns are often used in place of personal pronouns for emphasis or to indicate familiarity with people or things. They are usually placed at or near the beginning of the sentence. The demonstrative pronouns are identical to the relative pronouns.

Kennst du **Michael Schauer?**	—Ja, **den** kenne ich sehr gut.
Wie geht es **deinen Eltern** jetzt?	—**Denen** geht's gut.

2.5 *Der-* and *ein-*words as pronouns

Like the demonstrative pronouns, other **der**-words can also function as pronouns.

Welches Bild gefällt dir besser - **dieses** oder **jenes**?　　—**Dieses** finde ich besser.

Dieser Wagen ist toll!　　　　　—**Welchen** meinst du?

Ein-words can function as pronouns as well. In this usage they take the same endings as **der**-words.

	MASC.	FEM.	NEUT.	PL.
NOMINATIVE	meiner	meine	mein(e)s[6]	meine
ACCUSATIVE	meinen	meine	mein(e)s	meine
DATIVE	meinem	meiner	meinem	meinen
GENITIVE[7]	mein(e)s	meiner	mein(e)s	meiner

Kannst du mir einen Bleistift leihen? Ich habe **meinen** vergessen.
Hast du ein Auto? Leider habe ich **keins**.

2.6 Reflexive pronouns

Reflexive pronouns refer back to the subject of the sentence. Their English equivalents often use *-self* or *-selves*: *I cut myself.*

Some German verbs require reflexive pronouns in the dative, others in the accusative, some in either, depending on the circumstances. The reflexive pronouns are the same in both dative and accusative, except for first and second person singular.

		ACCUSATIVE	DATIVE
SINGULAR	ich	mich	mir
	du	dich	dir
	er/sie/es	sich	sich
PLURAL	wir	uns	uns
	ihr	euch	euch
	sie	sich	sich
SINGULAR AND PLURAL	Sie	sich	sich

---

[6]In conversation, the **e** is usually omitted: **Das ist meins**.

[7]These forms are rarely used.

An accusative reflexive pronoun is used when it functions as the direct object.

Hast du **dich** schon gewaschen?
Have you already washed up?

A dative reflexive pronoun is used when it functions as an indirect object.

Das kann ich **mir** kaum vorstellen.
I can scarcely imagine that.

Some verbs can take either accusative or dative reflexive pronouns, depending on whether the sentence already contains a direct object. (See also Section 3.9 on reflexive verbs.)

Ich ziehe **mich** an.   *I'm getting dressed.*
Ich ziehe **mir** die Schuhe an.   *I'm putting my shoes on.*

Reflexive pronouns are often used with the definite article to refer to parts of the body and to clothing.

Ich habe **mir** die Hände gewaschen.   *I washed my hands.*

Reflexive pronouns can also be used to indicate reciprocity: *each other.* If there is a possibility of ambiguity, then **einander** may be used instead.

Sie kritisieren **sich**.   *They criticize themselves* or *They criticize each other.*
Sie kritisieren **einander**.   *They criticize each other.*

2.7 Indefinite personal pronouns

The most frequently used indefinite personal pronouns are **man** (*one*), **jeder[mann]** (*everybody, everyone*), **jemand** (*somebody, someone*), and **niemand** (*nobody, no one*). Their declensions are:

NOM.	man	jedermann (jeder)[8]	jemand[9]	niemand
ACC.	einen	jedermann (jeden)	jemand(en)	niemand(en)
DAT.	einem	jedermann (jedem)	jemand(em)	niemand(em)
GEN.	eines	jedermanns (jedes)	jemand(es)	niemand(es)

These four pronouns refer to both males and females, but they are masculine in form.

Kennst du **jemand**, der mir   *Do you know someone who can help me?*
helfen kann?

The indefinite pronouns that refer to things and ideas—not people—are **alles, etwas, nichts, vieles,** etc. See Section 2.3 on relative pronouns (use of **was**).

---

[8]Although **jedermann** and **jeder** are interchangeable, **jeder** is much more common.

[9]The personal endings on **jemand** and **niemand** are most often omitted.

2.8 Interrogative pronouns

wer, was

The declensions of these interrogative pronouns are:

	PEOPLE	OBJECTS
NOM.	wer	was
ACC.	wen	was
DAT.	wem	was[10]
GEN.	wessen	-----

Wessen Computer ist das?   *Whose computer is this?*

Wen hast du auf deiner Reise   *Who(m) did you visit on your trip and what*
besucht und **was** hast du gesehen?   *did you see?*

welcher

The interrogative pronoun **welcher** (*which*) is declined like the **der**-words.

Aus **welchem** Land kommt   *What country does your grandmother*
deine Großmutter?   *come from?*

was für (ein)

The phrase **was für ein** may be used in either a question or an exclamation. The **ein** in **was für ein** is declined according to the role of the following noun in the sentence; it is not affected by the preposition **für**.

Was für einen Hut hat er?
What kind of hat does he have?

Was für Bücher liest du gern?
What kind of books do you like to read?

Was für ein schöner Tag!
What a beautiful day!

---

[10]The use of **was** with a dative preposition is rare.

3. Verbs

3.1 Overview of verbs

Indicative
  Present tense
  Past tenses
  Future tenses
  Imperative
  Subjunctive
    Subjunctive I
    Subjunctive II

Passive voice
Verb prefixes
Special verbs
Modal auxiliaries
Reflexives
Impersonal verbs
Verbs ending in -**ieren**
können, wissen, kennen

3.2 Indicative: present tense

Forms

The present tense is usually formed by adding the personal endings to the infinitive stem.

SINGEN: STEM = *SING-*	
ich sing**e**	wir sing**en**
du sing**st**	ihr sing**t**
er, sie, es sing**t**	sie sing**en**
Sie sing**en**	

Some verbs with **a**, **au**, or **e** stem vowels undergo stem-vowel changes in the **du** and **er/sie/es** forms. The vowels **a** and **au** become **ä** and **äu** respectively, and **e** becomes **i** or **ie**.

TRAGEN	
ich trage	wir tragen
du trägst	ihr tragt
er, sie, es trägt	sie tragen
Sie tragen	

SPRECHEN	
ich spreche	wir sprechen
du sprichst	ihr sprecht
er, sie, es spricht	sie sprechen
Sie sprechen	

It is important to memorize these changes when you learn the verbs themselves. The vowel change is always listed in the vocabulary of your text and in dictionaries.

Note the following variations.

	HEISSEN	ARBEITEN	ATMEN	TUN	SAMMELN
ich	heiße	arbeite	atme	tue	samm(e)le[d]
du	heißt[a]	arbeitest[b]	atmest[b]	tust	sammelst
er, sie, es	heißt	arbeitet[b]	atmet[b]	tut	sammelt
wir	heißen	arbeiten	atmen	tun[c]	sammeln[c]
ihr	heißt	arbeitet[b]	atmet[b]	tut	sammelt
sie, Sie	heißen	arbeiten	atmen	tun[c]	sammeln[c]

[a] If the verb stem ends in -**s**, -**ß**, -**x**, or -**z**, the **s** of the **du**-ending is omitted.

[b] If the verb stem ends in -**d**, -**t**, or -**m** or -**n** preceded by a consonant other than **l** or **r**, to facilitate pronunciation an **e** is inserted between the stem and the personal ending in the **du**, **er/sie/es**, and **ihr** forms.

[c] If the verb stem ends in just -**n** rather than -**en**, then the personal endings of the **wir** and **sie/Sie** forms are simply -**n**.

[d] If the stem ends in -**eln**, the **e** of the **ich** form personal ending is often dropped.

Uses of the present tense

The German present tense has only one form; it is the equivalent of all three possible forms in English.

ich singe
$$\begin{cases} I \ sing \\ I \ am \ singing \\ I \ do \ sing \end{cases}$$

The present tense is often used together with an adverb to indicate the future.

Morgen **gehe** ich in die Stadt.   *Tomorrow I will go into town.*

With **seit**, **schon**, or **schon seit,** the present tense can also indicate an action begun in the past and continuing in the present.

Ich wohne **seit** drei Jahren hier.   *I have lived here for three years.*

3.3 Past tenses

Principal parts and verb types: overview

Every German verb has three principal parts consisting of the infinitive, the third person simple past (imperfect), and the past participle. For example, the three principal parts of **trinken** are **trinken, trank, getrunken** (compare English *drink, drank, drunk*). Depending on how they form their principal parts, German verbs are classified as regular (or weak), irregular (strong), or mixed (irregular weak).

German regular verbs are similar to English regular verbs; there is no stem change, and they follow predictable patterns: **spielen, spielte, gespielt** (*play, played, played*).

Irregular verbs in German always undergo a stem-vowel change in the simple past forms and often in the past participle as well, as is the case with many irregular English verbs: **singen, sang, gesungen** (*sing, sang, sung*). The principal parts of these verbs must be memorized.

With mixed verbs, a stem vowel change occurs, as with irregular verbs, but the endings and suffixes correspond to those of the regular verbs (*to burn*: **brennen, brannte, gebrannt**).

The three past tenses

German has three tenses to indicate past time or events that have taken place in the past. They are the simple past (imperfect), the conversational past (present perfect), and the past perfect. The uses of these tenses do not always coincide with their uses in English.

Simple past (imperfect)

The simple past is most frequently used for narration or description of a situation; it occurs primarily in written German. The simple past of **haben, sein** and the modal auxiliaries (**dürfen, können, mögen, müssen, sollen, wollen**) are commonly used in conversation.

Simple past: regular verbs

Regular verbs add the suffix -t and the personal endings to the stem. An -e- may be inserted to facilitate pronunciation.

HOFFEN			
ich hoffte	*I hoped*	wir hofften	*we hoped*
du hofftest	*you hoped*	ihr hofftet	*you hoped*
er, sie, es hoffte	*he, she, it hoped*	sie hofften	*they hoped*
	Sie hofften	*you hoped*	

ANTWORTEN			
ich antwortete	*I answered*	wir antworteten	*we answered*
du antwortetest	*you answered*	ihr antwortetet	*you answered*
er, sie, es antwortete	*he, she, it answered*	sie antworteten	*they answered*
	Sie antworteten	*you answered*	

Haben is also a regular verb, but it has a consonant change in the simple past: **hatte.**

Simple past: irregular verbs

Irregular German verbs change their stem vowel in the simple past tense, and there is sometimes a consonant change as well. The personal endings are the same as in the present tense, except that the **ich** and **er/sie/es** forms do not take an ending at all, and there is no -**e**- in the **du** and **ihr** forms.

SINGEN	
ich sang	wir sang**en**
du sang**st**	ihr sang**t**
er, sie, es sang	sie sang**en**
Sie sang**en**	

GEHEN	
ich ging	wir ging**en**
du ging**st**	ihr ging**t**
er, sie, es ging	sie ging**en**
Sie ging**en**	

Simple past: mixed verbs

There are only seven mixed verbs: **brennen, bringen, denken, kennen, nennen, rennen,** and **wissen**. Like the irregular verbs, they undergo a stem-vowel change; but like the regular verbs, they use the -**t** suffix. A few of these verbs undergo a consonant change as well. The simple past of modal verbs is also formed in this way.

DENKEN	
ich dachte	wir dachten
du dachtest	ihr dachtet
er, sie, es dachte	sie dachten
Sie dachten	

DÜRFEN	
ich durfte	wir durften
du durftest	ihr durftet
er, sie es durfte	sie durften
Sie durften	

Conversational past (present perfect)

The present perfect tense is often called the *conversational past*, as it is used frequently in everyday speech. Both the conversational past and the simple past may be translated by a variety of English equivalents.

ich habe gespielt
ich spielte
{
I played
I have played
I did play
I used to play

The present perfect tense consists of an auxiliary verb (**haben** or **sein**) and the past participle of the main verb.

LERNEN		GEHEN	
ich habe gelernt	wir haben gelernt	ich bin gegangen	wir sind gegangen
du hast gelernt	ihr habt gelernt	du bist gegangen	ihr seid gegangen
er, sie, es hat gelernt	sie haben gelernt	er, sie, es ist gegangen	sie sind gegangen
Sie haben gelernt		Sie sind gegangen	

The more common auxiliary is **haben**. The auxiliary **sein** is used for intransitive verbs[11] that express a change of place or condition (**gehen, fliegen, werden, sterben**), as well as the verbs **bleiben, gelingen, geschehen, passieren**, and **sein**.

Conversational past: regular verbs

The past participle of regular verbs consists of the stem plus the prefix **ge-** and the suffix **-t** or **-et: ich bin gewandert, ich habe gearbeitet.**

N O T E ———————————————————————————————————

■ The prefix **ge-** is not used if the verb has an inseparable prefix. With separable prefix verbs, the **ge-** prefix is inserted between the prefix and the verb stem.

Sie haben die Arbeit **übersetzt.**   *They translated the work.*
Wir haben die Tür **aufgemacht.**   *We opened the door.*

■ The prefix **ge-** is not used for verbs whose infinitive ends with **-ieren.**

Sie hat Biologie **studiert.**   *She studied biology.*

Conversational past: irregular verbs

The past participle of irregular verbs consists of the perfect stem plus the prefix **ge-** and the suffix **-en: ich habe gesprochen, ich bin gelaufen.**

N O T E ———————————————————————————————————

The prefix **ge-** is omitted if the verb has an inseparable prefix. If it has a separable prefix, the **ge-** is inserted between the prefix and the verb stem.

Wir haben sie nicht **verstanden.**   *We didn't understand them.*
Warum sind Sie nicht **mitgekommen?**   *Why didn't you come along?*

---

[11]Intransitive verbs are verbs that do not take a direct object. Some verbs may be used either transitively or intransitively: **Er hat das Auto gefahren** (transitive); **Er ist in die Stadt gefahren** (intransitive).

Conversational past: mixed verbs

The past participle of mixed verbs consists of the perfect stem plus the prefix **ge-** and the suffix -t: **ich habe gewußt, ich bin gerannt.**

Past perfect

The past perfect in German has the same function as in English: It indicates that one event in the past precedes another past event.

*When we moved to Germany, we **had** already lived in many other countries.*

The past perfect tense is formed with the simple past tense of the auxiliary verb **haben** or **sein** and the past participle of the main verb.

BLEIBEN	
ich war geblieben	wir waren geblieben
du warst geblieben	ihr wart geblieben
er, sie, es war geblieben	sie waren geblieben
Sie waren geblieben	

WOHNEN	
ich hatte gewohnt	wir hatten gewohnt
du hattest gewohnt	ihr hattet gewohnt
er, sie, es hatte gewohnt	sie hatten gewohnt
Sie hatten gewohnt	

3.4 Future tenses

Future

The future tense is formed with the present tense of the auxiliary verb **werden** plus the infinitive of the main verb.

GEBEN			
ich werde geben	*I will give*	wir werden geben	*we will give*
du wirst geben	*you will give*	ihr werdet geben	*you will give*
er, sie, es wird geben	*he, she, it will give*	sie werden geben	*they will give*
Sie werden geben	*you will give*		

The future tense is used less frequently in German than in English, as the present tense with an adverb often indicates future time instead (see Section 3.2, Uses of the present tense). The future tense is used, however, when the time frame would otherwise be unclear, or when the speaker wishes to emphasize that something definitely will take place.

The future may also be used with **schon** or **wohl** to express probability.

Das wird sie **schon** wissen. ⎫
Das wird sie **wohl** wissen. ⎭   *She probably knows that.*

Future perfect

The future perfect is used only infrequently in German, usually to express past probability—i.e., the idea that something has already taken place. The future perfect is formed with the present tense of the auxiliary **werden** plus the past participle of the main verb and the infinitive **haben** or **sein**. Probability is most often indicated by **schon** or **wohl**.

Bis morgen **wird** sie das Buch wohl schon **gelesen** haben.
She will probably have read the book by tomorrow.

Bis wir ankommen, **wird** der Zug wohl **abgefahren** sein.
By the time we get there, the train will probably have departed.

3.5 Imperative

The German imperative has four different forms.

1. The imperative for the polite form **Sie** is identical to its present tense form, except that the verb precedes the pronoun. Frequently an exclamation point is added at the end of the command.

   Kommen Sie! Gehen Sie! Sehen Sie!

2. The imperative for the second person familiar singular (**du**) is formed by adding an optional -e to the infinitive stem.[12]

   Komm(e)! Warte!

   Irregular verbs with the stem-vowel change **e → i** or **e → ie** retain this change in the imperative;[13] verbs with the change **a → ä** or **au → äu** do not. Irregular verbs that change their stem vowel from **e** to **i** or **ie** never add the suffix -e.

   Gib! Sieh! Lauf(e)!

---

[12]The **e** is usually omitted in everyday speech; however, it must be used if the verb stem ends in **-t, -d, -ig**, or **m** or **n** preceded by a consonant other than **l** or **r**.

[13]**Werden** is an exception: **Er wird nicht krank**; but: **Werde nicht krank!**

3. The imperative for the second person familiar plural (**ihr**) is identical to its present tense form; however, the personal pronoun **ihr** is omitted.

Kommt! Gebt! Seht!

4. The imperative for the first person plural (**wir**) is identical to its present tense form; however, the verb precedes the pronoun. The English equivalent is *Let's....*

Kommen wir! Gehen wir! Sehen wir!

The imperative of **sein** is irregular: **Sei! Seid! Seien Sie! Seien wir!**

3.6 Subjunctive

While the indicative expresses facts and actual events, the subjunctive usually deals with hypothetical or unreal situations.

INDICATIVE:	*I am going skiing.*
SUBJUNCTIVE:	*If there **were** snow, I **would go** skiing.*

In German, there are two types of subjunctive.

Subjunctive I

Subjunctive I is used most often for indirect discourse (*He said that she will come tomorrow*). It is most common in formal situations such as news broadcasts, official statements, and literary works. Use of the subjunctive implies that the speaker cannot vouch for the truth of the statement, but is only repeating what someone else has said.

Subjunctive I is formed with the infinitive stem plus the subjunctive endings.[14]

FAHREN	
ich fahre	wir fahren
du fahrest	ihr fahret
er, sie, es fahre	sie fahren
Sie fahren	

Note that the **ich**, **wir**, and **sie/Sie** forms are the same as the present tense indicative. When Subjunctive I and the indicative are identical, Subjunctive I is never used. (Subjunctive II is usually substituted instead.) Furthermore, the **du** and **ihr** forms are considered stilted and are no longer used. Therefore only the **er/sie/es** form occurs with any frequency.

---

[14]Subjunctive I is so named because it is based on the first principal part of the verb (the infinitive). Subjunctive II is based on the second principal part.

In Subjunctive I, the verb **sein** does not take endings in the first and third persons singular: **ich sei, er sei.**

───

SUBJUNCTIVE I IN INDIRECT DISCOURSE: Die Journalistin sagt, der Präsident **sei** krank.
The journalist says the president is sick.

For additional examples, see the Section 3.6 on Indirect discourse.

Subjunctive I is also used in certain wishes and commands in the third person as follows:

COMMAND: Man **fahre** nicht über die gelbe Linie!
One should not cross the yellow line.

WISH: Gott **schütze** die Königin!
God save the Queen!

Subjunctive II (conditional)

Subjunctive II is used for hypothetical or contrary-to-fact conditions, for wishes and polite requests, and for indirect discourse. Subjunctive II consists of the simple past stem plus the subjunctive endings. The simple past stem of irregular verbs and mixed verbs takes an umlaut whenever possible (i.e., with the vowels **a, o, u**). Four of the mixed verbs (**brennen, kennen, nennen, rennen**) use **e** instead of an umlaut.

	SPAREN (*to save*): SPARTE	FAHREN: FUHR	KENNEN: KANNTE
ich	sparte	führe	kennte
du	spartest	führest	kenntest
er, sie, es	sparte	führe	kennte
wir	sparten	führen	kennten
ihr	spartet	führet	kenntet
sie, Sie	sparten	führen	kennten

Note that the Subjunctive II forms of regular verbs are identical to the past tense indicative. For this reason the **würde**-construction is usually used instead.

The *würde*-construction

Contrary-to-fact conditions can also be expressed by using the **würde**-construction. This consists of a conjugated form of **werden** plus the infinitive of the main verb; it corresponds to English *would…*

For any verb, **würde** + infinitive and the Subjunctive II form have the same meaning.

SUBJUNCTIVE **II**:	Wenn ich genug Geld **hätte,** flöge ich dahin.	*If I had enough money, I would fly there.*
würde + INFINITIVE:	Wenn ich genug Geld **hätte,** würde ich dahin **fliegen.**[15]	

Würde + infinitive is used more frequently than Subjunctive II in spoken German, except for **sein** (**wäre**), **haben** (**hätte**), **werden** (**würde**), **wissen** (**wüßte**), the modals, and a few other common verbs.

Subjunctive II and the **würde**-construction are frequently used as follows:

CONDITIONS AND CONCLUSIONS:	Wenn ich Zeit **hätte, würde** ich **mitfahren.** *If I had time, I would go along.*
CONDITIONS WITH NO STATED CONCLUSION:	Das **würde** ich nicht **machen!** *I wouldn't do that!*
WISHES:	Wenn es nur sonnig **wäre!** *If only it were sunny!*
POLITE REQUESTS:	**Würden** Sie bitte das Fenster **aufmachen?** *Would you please open the window?*
SUPPOSITIONS WITH *ALS OB* OR *ALS WENN:*	Du siehst aus, **als ob** du zuviel Arbeit **hättest.** *You look as though you had too much work.*
INDIRECT DISCOURSE:	Das Mädchen sagte, es **könnte** alles selbst machen. *The girl said she could do everything by herself.*

---

[15]Until recently, the use of **würde** in the **wenn**-clause was considered poor style. This is no longer necessarily the case.

Past subjunctive II

The past tense of Subjunctive II is formed by the Subjuntive II form of the auxiliary **haben** or **sein** and the past participle of the main verb.

FAHREN	
ich wäre gefahren	wir wären gefahren
du wärest gefahren	ihr wäret gefahren
er, sie, es wäre gefahren	sie wären gefahren
Sie wären gefahren	

HOFFEN	
ich hätte gehofft	wir hätten gehofft
du hättest gehofft	ihr hättet gehofft
er, sie, es hätte gehofft	sie hätten gehofft
Sie hätten gehofft	

Wenn ich genug Geld **gehabt hätte, wäre** ich dahin **geflogen.**
If I had had enough money, I would have flown there.

Indirect discourse

Subjunctive I, Subjunctive II, and the **würde**-conditional may all be used to express indirect discourse. Subjunctive I is primarily used in written German and in formal situations such as news broadcasts. Subjunctive II is used in general conversation. In all cases, ambiguity should be avoided. Subjunctive II replaces Subjunctive I if Subjunctive I could be confused with the present tense indicative; **würde** + infinitive replaces Subjunctive II if Subjunctive II could be confused with the past tense indicative.

Indirect statement

SUBJUNCTIVE I:	Er sagte, daß sie das Auto reparieren. (*ambiguous*)
SUBJUNCTIVE II:	Er sagte, daß sie das Auto reparierten. (*ambiguous*)
WÜRDE + INFINITIVE:	Er sagte, daß sie das Auto reparieren **würden.**
	He said that they would repair the car.

Indirect question

SUBJUNCTIVE I:	Er fragte, wann sie das Auto reparierten. (*ambiguous*)
SUBJUNCTIVE II:	Er fragte, wann sie das Auto repariert **hätten.**
	He asked when they had repaired the car.

N O T E ———————————————————————

Since the past subjunctive is not at all ambiguous, there is no past form of the **würde**-construction.

Study the following examples of how Subjunctive I and Subjunctive II are used in indirect discourse. Note that the tense of the introductory verb (**sagt, behauptete,** etc.) has no effect on the tense of the quoted verb.

PRESENT TENSE:	"Ich finde den Film ausgezeichnet."
	Er sagt, daß er den Film ausgezeichnet finde/fände.
	He says that he thinks the film is excellent.
ALL PAST TENSES:	"Ich bin/war erfolgreich gewesen."
	OR: "Ich war erfolgreich."
	Er hat behauptet, er **sei/wäre** erfolgreich **gewesen**.
	He maintained that he was successful.
	"Ich **habe/hatte** meine Tasche verloren."
	OR: "Ich verlor meine Tasche."
	Sie erklärte, sie **habe/hätte** ihre Tasche **verloren**.
	She explained that she had lost her purse.
FUTURE TENSE:	"Ich werde bald kommen."
	Er meinte, daß er bald **kommen werde/würde**.
	He said that he would come soon.
DIRECT QUESTIONS:	"Hast du schon gegessen?"
	Sie wollte wissen, ob er schon **gegessen habe/hätte**.
	She wanted to know whether he had eaten yet.
COMMANDS:	"Komm her!"
	Er sagte, sie **solle/sollte/soll herkommen**.[16]
	He told her to come here.

3.7 Passive voice

In both German and English, sentences are in either of two voices: active or passive. In the active voice, the focus is on the subject—the person or thing who performs the action. In the passive voice, the focus is on the recipient of the action. When a sentence is changed from the active to the passive voice, the direct object becomes the subject, and the subject becomes the so-called agent.

	SUBJECT	DIR. OBJ.
ACTIVE:	The best-selling author is writing	a new book.

	SUBJECT	AGENT
PASSIVE:	A new book is being written	by the best-selling author.

---

[16]Note that the indicative (**soll**) may be used here.

In German, the passive voice is formed with the auxiliary **werden** plus the past participle of the main verb. If the source of action (the agent) is a living being, the preposition **von** (+ dative case) is used; if the agent is a means, the preposition **durch** (+ accusative case) is used.

Das Gebäude **wird** von dem jungen Architekten **gebaut**.	*The building is being built by the young architect.*
Das Haus **wurde** durch Feuer **zerstört**.	*The house was destroyed by fire.*

Tenses of the passive voice

PRESENT	es **wird gebaut**	*it is being built*
SIMPLE PAST	es **wurde gebaut**	*it was (being) built*
CONVERSATIONAL PAST	es **ist gebaut worden**	*it has been built*
PAST PERFECT	es **war gebaut worden**	*it had been built*
FUTURE	es **wird gebaut werden**	*it will be built*
FUTURE PERFECT	es **wird gebaut worden sein**	*it will have been built*

NOTE ——

- The past participle of the auxiliary **werden** is **worden**, whereas the past participle of the verb **werden** (*to become*) is **geworden**.
- The perfect tenses of the passive are always formed with the auxiliary **sein** rather than **haben**.

Passive sentences always contain a form of the verb **werden**. In similar sentences, a state or condition is expressed with a form of **sein** plus the past participle; this construction is frequently referred to as the *statal passive* or *false passive*. In such situations the participle actually functions as an adjective.

PASSIVE:	Die Tür **wird geschlossen**.	*The door is being closed.*
STATAL PASSIVE:	Die Tür **ist geschlossen**.	*The door is closed.*

Some passive sentences have no real subject.

Gestern **wurde gefeiert**.	*Yesterday there was a celebration.*
Es **wurde** viel **getanzt**.	*There was a lot of dancing.*

The passive can be avoided by using the following constructions:

MAN:	Hier wird Deutsch gesprochen. → Hier spricht **man** Deutsch.
SEIN + ZU + INFINITIVE:	Die Straße kann schwer gefunden werden. → Die Straße **ist** schwer **zu finden**.
SICH LASSEN:	Das Brot wird leicht geschnitten.→ Das Brot **läßt sich** leicht schneiden.
REFLEXIVE:	Diese Verben werden schnell gelernt. → Diese Verben **lernen sich** schnell.

3.8 Verb prefixes

Many German verbs have prefixes that change or modify their meaning. There are two different types of prefixes: separable and inseparable.

Inseparable prefixes

The inseparable prefixes are **be-, emp-, ent-, er-, ge-, miß-, ver-, zer-**. These prefixes never separate from the verb, and their past participles do not add the past participle prefix **ge-**.

Er hat sie **miß**verstanden.   *He misunderstood her.*

Separable prefixes

Separable prefixes are those that can stand alone; they are most often prepositions or adverbs, but may sometimes be nouns or other verbs. In independent clauses in the present tense, the simple past tense, and the imperative mood, the prefix separates from the verb stem and moves to final position. In the perfect tenses, the **ge-** is inserted between the prefix and the main verb.

In dependent clauses, the prefix remains attached to the main verb.

INDEPENDENT CLAUSES: Er **geht** jetzt **weg.**
Er **ging** gestern **weg.**
Gehen Sie jetzt **weg!**
Er ist gestern **weggegangen.**

DEPENDENT CLAUSE: Ich weiß, daß er **weggeht.**

In infinitive phrases with **zu**, the word **zu** appears between the prefix and the main verb.

Er beschloß, **wegzugehen.**   *He decided to leave.*

N O T E

A few prefixes may be either separable or inseparable, depending on their meaning. These prefixes are **durch-, über-, um-, unter-, wieder-,** and **wider-**. When they are used as separable prefixes, the verb has a more literal meaning; when they are used as inseparable prefixes, the verb has a more abstract meaning.

Er **setzte** die Leute **über.**   *He ferried the people across.*
Er **übersetzte** das Buch.   *He translated the book.*

3.9 Special verbs

Modal verbs

Modal verbs express an attitude about an action; they are usually accompanied by another verb (a dependent infinitive) that expresses the action itself.[17] German has six modal verbs.

dürfen	*to be allowed, may*	**müssen**	*to have to, must*
können	*to be able to, can*	**sollen**	*to be supposed to, ought*
mögen	*to like (to)*	**wollen**	*to want*

Er **will** das Buch lesen.	*He wants to read the book.*
Ich **muß** jetzt meine Hausaufgaben machen.	*I have to do my homework now.*

NOTE ────────────────────────────────────

Note the following variations in usage:

- **Mögen.** In the present tense, the subjunctive of **mögen** is frequently used in polite requests.

Ich **möchte** eine Tasse Kaffee.	*I would like a cup of coffee.*

  Otherwise **mögen** is used most often in negative statements and in questions, usually with no dependent infinitive.

  Magst du diesen Kuchen?—Nein, ich **mag** ihn nicht.

- **Dürfen** and **müssen.** To express English *must not*, use **nicht dürfen.**

Heute **muß** ich **nicht** einkaufen gehen.	*Today I don't have to go shopping.*
Heute **darf** ich **nicht** einkaufen gehen.	*Today I must not (am not allowed to) go shopping.*

- **Wollen.** To say that you want someone to do something, use **wollen** plus a **daß**-clause.

Er **will**, daß ich ihm helfe.	*He wants me to help him.*

Tenses of modals

1. The present tense of the modal verbs is irregular.

---

[17]Sometimes modals are used without a dependent infinitive when the missing verb is clearly understood; this usually occurs with **fahren, gehen, machen,** and **tun: Mußt du jetzt nach Hause (gehen)?**

	DÜRFEN	KÖNNEN	MÖGEN	MÜSSEN	SOLLEN	WOLLEN
ich	darf	kann	mag	muß	soll	will
du	darfst	kannst	magst	mußt	sollst	willst
er, sie, es	darf	kann	mag	muß	soll	will
wir	dürfen	können	mögen	müssen	sollen	wollen
ihr	dürft	könnt	mögt	müßt	sollt	wollt
sie, Sie	dürfen	können	mögen	müssen	sollen	wollen

2. The simple past of modal verbs is similar to that of the weak verbs, with slight irregularities: **ich durfte, ich konnte, ich mochte, ich mußte, ich sollte, ich wollte.**

3. The perfect tenses are formed as follows: When a modal has a dependent infinitive, the past participle of the modal is the same as its infinitive. When there is no dependent infinitive, the past participle is formed like that of a weak verb.

DEPENDENT INFINITIVE: Ich habe reisen **dürfen**.   *I was allowed to travel.*
NO DEPENDENT INFINITIVE: Ich habe sie immer **gemocht**.   *I always liked her.*

4. The future tense is also formed with a double infinitive, as follows:

Ich werde früh **aufstehen müssen**.   *I will have to get up early.*

Reflexive verbs

A number of German verbs require a reflexive pronoun; some of them govern the dative case, others the accusative. (See also the Section 2.6 on reflexive pronouns.)

DATIVE: Ich stelle **mir** das sehr interessant vor.
I imagine that to be very interesting.

ACCUSATIVE: Darf ich **mich** bitte vorstellen?
May I please introduce myself?

In addition, nearly any transitive verb[18] can be used reflexively. Note the following examples:

NON-REFLEXIVE	REFLEXIVE
Er **wäscht** das Auto.	Er **wäscht sich**.
He is washing the car.	*He is washing himself.*
Dieses Problem **ärgert mich**.	Ich **ärgere mich** darüber.
This problem annoys me.	*I am annoyed about it.*
Du **erinnerst mich** an meinen Bruder.	Ich **erinnere mich** an ihn.
You remind me of my brother.	*I remember him.*

---

[18]Reminder: a transitive verb is one that takes a direct object.

German has many reflexive verbs whose English equivalents are not reflexive; a few common ones are:

sich amüsieren	*to have fun*	**sich erkälten**	*to catch a cold*
sich anziehen	*to get dressed*	**sich setzen**	*to sit down*
sich beeilen	*to hurry*		

Impersonal verbs

Verbs that take only the impersonal pronoun **es** as their subject are called impersonal verbs.

Es regnet.   *It is raining.*

N O T E ———————————————————————

Es is also used in the idiomatic expression **es gibt** (see Section 2.1 on Personal pronouns).

Verbs ending in -*ieren*

Verbs ending in -**ieren** do not take the past participle prefix **ge-**.

Er hat lange **regiert**.   *He reigned for a long time.*

The verbs *können, kennen, wissen*

All three of these verbs can be translated as *to know*, but they are not interchangeable.

As a modal verb, **können** means *to be able to, can*. It can also indicate that one knows how to do something, or it can be used independently to indicate that one knows a language.

Karsten **kann** sehr gut kochen.   *Karsten knows how to (can) cook very well.*
Sie **kann** gut Deutsch.   *She knows German well; she can speak German well.*

The verb **kennen** denotes acquaintance.

Er **kennt** alle.   *He knows everyone.*

The verb **wissen** indicates factual knowledge.

Ich **weiß**, daß die Erde rund ist.   *I know that the earth is round.*

N O T E ————————————————

The principal parts of **wissen** are **wissen**, **wußte**, **gewußt**. It is conjugated irregularly in the present tense.

WISSEN	
ich weiß	wir wissen
du weißt	ihr wißt
er, sie, es weiß	sie wissen
Sie wissen	

4. Adjectives and adverbs

4.1 Adjectives

In German, all attributive adjectives—that is, adjectives that precede the noun they modify—take endings. There are two types of adjective endings: strong and weak.

Strong adjective endings

An adjective takes the so-called strong endings when it is not preceded either by a **der**-word or by an **ein**-word with an ending.[19] The strong endings are:

	MASCULINE	FEMININE	NEUTER	PLURAL
NOM.	großer	große	großes	große
ACC.	großen	große	großes	große
DAT.	großem	großer	großem	großen
GEN.	großen	großer	großen	großer

Note that these endings are the same as the **der**-word endings except for the masculine and neuter genitive.

Frische Brötchen schmecken toll!	*Fresh rolls taste great!*
Sein blauer Wagen scheint ganz neu zu sein.	*His blue car seems to be quite new.*
Bei schlechtem Wetter bleiben wir zu Hause.	*In bad weather we'll stay home.*

Weak adjective endings

An adjective takes the weak endings when it is preceded by an **ein**-word with an ending or by a **der**-word. The weak endings are:

	MASCULINE	FEMININE	NEUTER	PLURAL
NOM.	große	große	große	großen
ACC.	großen	große	große	großen
DAT.	großen	großen	großen	großen
GEN.	großen	großen	großen	großen

Dieser süße Saft schmeckt mir nicht.	*This sweet juice doesn't taste good.*
Meine Großmutter hat einen schönen Blumengarten.	*My grandmother has a beautiful flower garden.*

---

[19]The **ein**-words with no endings are the masculine nominative, the neuter nominative, and the neuter accusative (**ein**, **mein**, etc.). See the chart in Section 1.2 on Indefinite articles.

The principle behind strong and weak adjectives is basically a simple one: in every adjective-noun combination, one of the words must indicate gender or number and case. If a **der**-word or an **ein**-word ending is not present to convey this information, then the adjective itself must do so.

N O T E ————————————————————————————————

■ All attributive adjectives in a series take the same endings.

Hast du die schön**en** bunt**en** Blumen gesehen?

■ Predicate adjectives (those that follow the verbs **sein, werden,** or **bleiben**) are never declined.

Der Blumengarten ist **schön.**　　　*The flower garden is beautiful.*

Numerical adjectives

There are two types of numerical adjectives: definite (**alle** and **beide**) and indefinite (**andere, wenige, einige, mehrere, viele**). Both types are always plural.

The definite numerical adjectives function in the same way as **der**-words. Therefore any adjectives following them take weak endings, in this case **-en.**

Beid**e** neu**en** Filme haben mir gut gefallen.
I liked both new movies.

All**e** ausländisch**en** Studenten dürfen nach Berlin mitfahren.
All foreign students may go along to Berlin.

Adjectives that follow the indefinite numerical adjectives take the same endings as the numerical adjectives themselves.

In Hamburg habe ich die ander**en** neu**en** Theaterstücke gesehen.
In Hamburg I saw the other new plays.

(Since **andere** is preceded by a **der**-word, both adjectives take weak endings.)

Nur wenig**e** jung**e** Leute gehen oft in die Sauna.
Only a few young people go often to the sauna.

(Since **wenige** is unpreceded, both adjectives take strong endings.)

Adjectives used as nouns

Many German adjectives can be used as nouns. When this occurs, the adjectives must be capitalized, and they take the same adjective endings they would have taken if the missing nouns were present.

die blonde Frau → Kennst du die Blonde da?
Do you know that blond (woman)?

ein verwandter Mann → Ich habe einen Verwandten in Deutschland.
I have a (male) relative in Germany.

Neuter adjective nouns refer to abstract qualities; they often follow indefinite pronouns such as **etwas**, **nichts**, **vieles**, etc.

Heute ist nichts Interessantes passiert.   *Nothing interesting happened today.*
Das Wichtige kommt noch.   *The important thing is still to come.*

4.2 Comparative and superlative of adjectives and adverbs

In German, adverbs often have the same form as adjectives.[20]

ADJECTIVE:	Die Musik ist **laut**.	*The music is loud.*
ADVERB:	Sie spricht **laut**.	*She is speaking loudly.*

In both English and German, adjectives and adverbs have three degrees.

POSITIVE:	schön	*nice, pretty*
COMPARATIVE:	schöner	*nicer, prettier*
SUPERLATIVE:	schönst-	*nicest, prettiest*

The comparative of adjectives and adverbs is formed by adding **-er** to the positive form.

Der Volkswagen ist klein**er** als der Ford.

If the comparative form precedes the noun, it takes regular adjective endings as well.

Der Volkswagen war ein klein**er**er Wagen als der Ford.

The superlative of attributive adjectives is formed by adding **-st** to the positive form. The regular adjective endings are added as well.

Berlin ist die schön**ste** Stadt Deutschlands.

The superlative of predicate adjectives and of adverbs is formed with the word **am** and the suffix -**sten**.[21]

Die Nachtigall (*nightingale*) singt **am** schön**sten**.

---

[20]Reminder: an adverb is a word that modifies a verb, an adjective, or another adverb.

[21]Predicate adjectives may use either superlative form: **Dieses Haus ist am teuersten** = **Dieses Haus ist das teuerste**.

Note the following variations:

- Many monosyllabic adjectives and adverbs with stem-vowels **a**, **o**, or **u** are umlauted in the comparative and the superlative degrees: **jung, jünger, jüngst-**.

- To facilitate pronunciation, the superlative ending is expanded to -**est** when the adjective or adverb ends in -**d**, -**t**, -**s**, -**ß**, or **z**: **heiß, heißer, heißest-**; **kalt, kälter, kältest-**.[22]

- The following adjectives and adverbs form their comparitives and superlatives irregularly:

POSITIVE	COMPARATIVE	SUPERLATIVE
bald	eher	am ehesten
gern	lieber	am liebsten
gut	besser	best- / am besten
hoch, hoh	höher	höchst- / am höchsten
nah	näher	nächst- / am nächsten
viele	mehr	meist- / am meisten

Comparisons to other people or things are expressed with the positive form and (**nicht**) **so ... wie** or the comparative form and **als**.

Thomas ist (nicht) **so** groß **wie** Peter.
Peter ist **größer als** Thomas.

---

[22]**Groß** is an exception: **groß, größer, größt-**.

5. Word order and conjunctions

5.1 Word order in sentences

German sentences have three kinds of word order: normal, inverted, and dependent.

Normal word order

In normal word order, the subject (S) and its modifiers are followed by the inflected verb (V) and its modifiers.

      (S) (V)
Der alte Mann hat viel erlebt.
The old man has experienced much.

Inverted word order

In inverted word order, the inflected verb (V) precedes the subject (S) and its modifiers. Inverted word order is used in questions and in sentences beginning with an element other than the subject.

 (V) (S)
Kauft er sich heute einen neuen Anzug?

      (V)   (S)
Morgen wird das Wetter wieder schön sein.

Dependent word order

Dependent word order occurs in dependent clauses—that is, clauses that cannot stand alone. They are introduced by subordinating conjunctions or relative pronouns (see Sections 5.3 and 2.3 respectively). The subordinating conjunction is followed by the subject (S) and its modifiers; the inflected verb (V) is in last position.

     SUB. CONJ. (S)   (V)
Der Vater verlangt, **daß** seine Kinder ihm gehorchen.

- All relative pronouns require dependent word order.

          (S)   (V)

  Das ist die Frau, die ich gestern kennengelernt habe.

- The dependent clause is set off from the main clause by a comma.

- In dependent clauses, the separable prefix is attached to the verb.

  Wissen Sie, wann der Zug **abfährt**?

- Dependent clauses may begin the complete sentence. In that case, the main clause begins with its inflected verb. Note that the sentence as a whole has inverted word order; the dependent clause simply functions as the first element.

  DEP. CLAUSE   (V) (S)

  Warum er so traurig ist, weiß ich nicht.

- In sentences with an inflected verb plus two infinitives (such as the perfect tenses of the modal verbs), the inflected verb precedes the infinitives.

          (S)   (V)

  Sie sagte, daß sie den Mann nicht hätte sehen können.
  She said that she had not been able to see the man.

5.2 Other points of word order

Time-manner-place

When a sentence contains several adverbs or adverbial expressions, they follow the sequence time-manner-place. General information precedes specific information.

              TIME   **MANNER**   **PLACE**

Ich fahre morgen um vier Uhr mit meinen Eltern nach Bremen.

Direct and indirect objects

Remember that a direct object receives the action of the verb and is in the accusative case; the indirect object is the person or thing to whom or for whom something is done and is in the dative case.

If the direct object is a noun, it follows the indirect object.

	IND. OBJ.	**DIR. OBJ.**
Er gibt	dem Kind	den Ball.
Er gibt	ihm	den Ball.

If the direct object is a pronoun, it precedes the indirect object.

	DIR. OBJ.	IND. OBJ.
Er gibt	ihn	dem Kind.
Er gibt	ihn	ihm.

Note that in all instances the pronoun precedes the noun.

Position of *nicht*

In German sentences, **nicht** usually follows:

1. **THE MAIN VERB:**	Er arbeitet **nicht**.
2. **THE DIRECT AND INDIRECT OBJECTS:**	Siehst du ihn **nicht**?
3. **SPECIFIC TIME EXPRESSIONS:**	Wir gehen heute **nicht** schwimmen.

Nicht may also precede a word that is emphasized; it is often used in conjunction with the expression **sondern**.

Sie ist **nicht** meine Mutter, **sondern** meine Tante.
She is not my mother, but (rather) my aunt.

Nicht precedes almost everything else.

1. **GENERAL TIME EXPRESSIONS:**	Wir gehen **nicht** oft schwimmen.
2. **ADVERBS:**	Sie tanzt **nicht** gern.
3. **PREDICATE NOMINATIVES:**	Er ist **nicht** mein Freund.
4. **PREDICATE ADJECTIVES:**	Das Kleid ist **nicht** schön.
5. **SEPARABLE PREFIXES:**	Warum kommst du morgen **nicht** vorbei?
6. **PAST PARTICIPLES:**	Das habe ich **nicht** gekauft.
7. **INFINITIVES:**	Ich kann das **nicht** verstehen.

5.3 Conjunctions

There are two types of conjunctions: coordinating and subordinating.

Coordinating conjunctions

Coordinating conjunctions connect two independent clauses. Both clauses have normal word order.

aber	*but*
denn	*because, for*
oder	*or*
sondern	*but (on the contrary)*
und	*and*

Ich gehe jetzt nach Hause, **denn** ich bin müde.

Although **aber** and **sondern** both mean *but*, they are not interchangeable. **Sondern** is used for elements that are mutually exclusive. Compare the following sentences:

Das Buch ist lang, **aber** es ist interessant.
Das Buch ist nicht interessant, **sondern** langweilig.

Subordinating conjunctions

Subordinating conjunctions connect a dependent clause to a main clause. Subordinating conjunctions are followed by dependent word order. (See also Section 5.1.)

als	*when*
als ob	*as if, as though*
bevor	*before*
bis	*until*
da	*since, because*
damit	*so that*
daß	*that*
ehe	*before*
falls	*in case*
nachdem	*after*
ob	*whether*
obgleich	
obschon	*although, even though*
obwohl	
seitdem	*since (time)*
sobald	*as soon as*
solange	*as long as*
sooft	*as often as*
während	*while*
weil	*because*
wenn	*when*
wenn auch	*even though*

Interrogative words may also function as subordinating conjunctions.

Er fragte uns, **wann** wir nach Hause kämen.

Although **als**, **wenn**, and **wann** all mean *when*, they are not interchangeable.

- **Als** refers to an event in the past.
  Als ich nach Wien fuhr, habe ich meinen Koffer verloren.
  Als ich in Zürich wohnte, hatte ich eine schöne Wohnung.

- **Wenn** can mean *when, whenever,* or *if.*
  Wenn ich nach Wien fahre, besuche ich den Dom.
  Whenever I go to Vienna, I visit the cathedral; or
  When I go to Vienna, I'll visit the cathedral.

- **Wann** is an interrogative.
  Wann fahren Sie nach Wien?

Two-part conjunctions

German, like English, also has several two-part conjunctions.

sowohl ... als auch	*both ... and*
nicht nur ... sondern auch	*not only ... but also*
entweder ... oder	*either ... or*
weder ... noch	*neither ... nor*

Ich kann *weder* Chinesisch *noch* Russisch.
Entweder ißt du deine Erbsen *oder* du gehst ins Zimmer![23]

---

[23]Word order with **entweder ... oder** may vary: the following sentence is equally correct:
Entweder du ißt deine Erbsen oder ...

6. Prepositions

There are four types of prepositions in German: those that take the dative, those that take the accusative, those that take either the dative or the accusative, and those that take the genitive.

6.1 Dative prepositions

The following prepositions take the dative case.

aus	*out of, of, from*
außer	*besides, except (for)*
bei	*with, near; at the home/place of*
entgegen	*towards*
gegenüber	*opposite*
mit	*with; by* (transportation)
nach	*after, to, according to*
seit	*since* (time)
von	*from, by, of, about*
zu	*to, at*

6.2 Accusative prepositions

The following prepositions always take the accusative case.

bis	*until, as far as*
durch	*through, by*
für	*for*
gegen	*against; toward* (time)
ohne	*without*
um	*around; about, at* (time)
wider	*against*

6.3 Dative or accusative prepositions

The following prepositions take either the dative or the accusative case, depending on their use within the sentence.

an	*at, to, on*	**über**	*over, above*
auf	*on, in, to, at*	**unter**	*under, among*
hinter	*behind*	**vor**	*in front of, before; ago*
in	*in, into, to*	**zwischen**	*between*
neben	*beside, next to*		

These prepositions take the dative case if time or location is expressed; they answer the question **Wo?** They take the accusative case if a destination or movement toward a destination is expressed, answering the question **Wohin?**

Das Ehepaar ging **in das** Restaurant.
The couple went into the restaurant.

Das Ehepaar saß **im** Restaurant.
The couple sat in the restaurant.

N O T E ———————————————————————————————

If neither location nor destination is clear, as in abstract meanings or idiomatic expressions, a dictionary will indicate the required preposition and case.

6.4 Genitive prepositions

The following prepositions always take the genitive case.

außerhalb	*outside of*
innerhalb	*inside of, within*
oberhalb	*above*
unterhalb	*below*
diesseits	*on this side of*
jenseits	*on that side of*
(an-)statt	*instead of*
trotz	*in spite of*
während	*during*
wegen	*because of*
um ... willen	*for the sake of*

N O T E ———————————————————————————————

In contemporary spoken German, **trotz** and **wegen** are often used with the dative case.

6.5 Contractions of prepositions

The following contractions are common in the dative and the accusative cases.

DATIVE	ACCUSATIVE
am = an dem	**ans** = an das
	aufs = auf das
beim = bei dem	
	durchs = durch das
	fürs = für das
im = in dem	**ins** = in das
	ums = um das
vom = von dem	
zum = zu dem	
zur = zu der	

6.6 *da-* and *wo-*compounds

In prepositional phrases in German, pronouns refer only to persons. To refer to things or ideas, a **da**-compound must be used.

Sie freut sich auf die Ferien. Sie freut sich **darauf**.
She is looking forward to vacation. She is looking forward to it.

Ich fahre mit dem Motorrad. Ich fahre **damit**.
I am riding the motorcycle. I am riding it.

BUT: Ich fahre mit meinem Bruder. Ich fahre **mit ihm**.
I'm going with my brother. I'm going with him.

Similarly, **wo**-compounds are usually used to ask about objects.

Womit fährst du? Ich fahre mit dem Motorrad.
What are you riding? I am riding the motorcycle.

BUT: Mit wem fährst du? Ich fahre **mit meinem** Bruder.

NOTE ────────────────────────────────

- **da**- and **wo**- become **dar**- and **wor**- if the following preposition begins with a vowel: **Sie freut sich darauf.**

- **da**- and **wo**- compounds occur only in the dative or accusative cases and only in reference to inanimate objects.

7. Numerals

CARDINAL NUMERALS

0 null
1 eins
2 zwei
3 drei
4 vier
5 fünf
6 sechs
7 sieben
8 acht
9 neun
10 zehn
11 elf
12 zwölf
13 dreizehn
14 vierzehn
15 fünfzehn
16 sechzehn
17 siebzehn
18 achtzehn
19 neunzehn
20 zwanzig
21 einundzwanzig
30 dreißig
40 vierzig
50 fünfzig
60 sechzig
70 siebzig
80 achtzig
90 neunzig
100 (ein)hundert
101 (ein)hundert(und)eins
200 zweihundert
1000 (ein)tausend
2000 zweitausend
1 000 000 eine Million
2 000 000 zwei Millionen
1 000 000 000 eine Milliarde

ORDINAL NUMERALS

1. der erste
2. der zweite
3. der dritte
4. der vierte
5. der fünfte
6. der sechste
7. der siebte (*less common:* der siebente)
8. der achte
9. der neunte
10. der zehnte
11. der elfte
12. der zwölfte
13. der dreizehnte
14. der vierzehnte
15. der fünfzehnte
16. der sechzehnte
17. der siebzehnte
18. der achtzehnte
19. der neunzehnte
20. der zwanzigste
21. der einundzwanzigste
30. der dreißigste
40. der vierzigste
50. der fünfzigste
60. der sechzigste
70. der siebzigste
80. der achtzigste
90. der neunzigste
100. der (ein)hundertste
101. der (ein)hundert(und)erste
200. der zweihundertste
1000. der tausendste
2000. der zweitausendste
1 000 000. der millionste
2 000 000. der zweimillionste
1 000 000 000. der milliardste

Note that the ordinal numbers are adjectives and take the usual adjective endings.

Heute feiert Oma ihren **achtzigsten** Geburtstag.

Fractions

Fractions use the suffix **-tel** (from 4 through 19) or **-stel** (from 20 on): **drei Viertel, ein Zwanzigstel**. The denominators of 2 and 3 are irregular: ½ - **ein halb**, ⅓ - **ein Drittel**.

N O T E ————————————————————————————————————

- Instead of the decimal point, German uses the decimal comma: 2,5 (**zwei Komma fünf**) = 2.5.

- In expressing *one and a half*, German-speakers say **anderthalb**. In counting other halves, for example *six and a half*, they will say **sechseinhalb**. *Half of* is often stated as **die Hälfte** + genitive or **die Hälfte von**: Ich habe **die Hälfte der Äpfel** gegessen.